WHY WRITE?

ALSO BY STEVEN PRESSFIELD

FICTION

The Legend of Bagger Vance
Gates of Fire
Tides of War
Last of the Amazons
The Virtues of War
The Afghan Campaign
Killing Rommel
The Profession
The Knowledge
36 Righteous Men (2019)

NONFICTION

The War of Art
The Warrior Ethos
Turning Pro
The Authentic Swing
Do the Work
The Lion's Gate
An American Jew
Nobody Wants to Read Your Sh*t
The Artist's Journey

WHY WRITE?

Meditations on Fame, Money, Self-Actualization and Other Stuff

STEVEN PRESSFIELD

A BLACK IRISH JAB
BLACK IRISH ENTERTAINMENT LLC

Black Irish Entertainment LLC
223 Egremont Plain Road
PMB 191
Egremont, MA 01230

For Information About Special
Discounts for Bulk Purchases,
Please Visit www.blackirishbooks.com

ISBN: 978-1-936891-26-9
Ebook: 978-1-936891-63-4

For David Y.B. Kaufmann

A NOTE TO THE READER

Unedited drafts of some of the materials within were first published as part of the "Writing Wednesdays" column on www.stevenpressfield.com.

About Black Irish Jabs

In the heat of battle against Resistance, when you're on the ropes and your guard begins to fall, you don't need a five-hundred-page treatise on the whys and wherefores of syntax or global story structure.

You need a shot of adrenaline to quickly remind you of storytelling's first principles.

That's what Black Irish Jabs are—short, laser-targeted and to the point pieces of professional craft advice to put Resistance where it belongs . . . back on its heels.

Now get back in the ring!

—Steven Pressfield and Shawn Coyne

1
WHAT IS SUCCESS?

I stumbled onto the website of a novelist I had never heard of. (He's probably never heard of me either.) What I saw there got me thinking.

The site was excellent. It displayed all fourteen of the novelist's books in "cover flow" format. They looked great. A couple had been published by HarperCollins, several others by Random House. The author was the real deal, a thoroughgoing pro with a body of work produced over decades.

I found myself thinking, *What if this excellent writer had never been published?*

Would we still think of him as a success?

(In other words, I started pondering the definition of "success" for a writer.)

Suppose, I said to myself ... suppose this writer had written all these novels, had had their covers designed impeccably, had their interiors laid out to the highest professional standards.

Suppose he could never find a publisher.

Suppose he self-published all fourteen of his novels.

Suppose his books had found a readership of several hundred, maybe a thousand or two. But never more.

Suppose he had died with that as the final tally.

Would we say he had "failed"?

Would we declare his writing life a waste?

[I'm assuming, for the sake of this exercise, that our writer had been able somehow to support himself and his family throughout his life or that, if he had been supported by someone else (like Theo van Gogh took care of Vincent), that was okay with him and with the person supporting him.]

Then I asked myself, *What if that was me?*

How would I feel about those fourteen books? Would I consider them an exercise in folly? Vanity? Demented self-indulgence?

Would I say to myself, "What's wrong with you? Why do you continue this enterprise of futility? Wake up! Get a job!"

Could I justify all that effort and somehow convince myself that it was worthy, that it had been an honorable use of my time on Earth?

It won't surprise you, if you're at all familiar with my thinking in this area, to hear that I would immediately answer yes.

Yes, I would consider that hypothetical writer a success.

I might even declare him a *spectacular* success.

No, his writing life was not wasted.

No, he had not squandered his time on the planet.

And yes, I would say the same if that writer were me.

My own real-life career is not that far off from this hypothetical. I wrote for seventeen years before I got my first dollar (a check for $3,500 for an option on a screenplay that never came near getting made). I wrote for twenty-eight years before my first novel was published.

What, then, constitutes success for a writer? Is it money? Sales? Recognition? Is it "expressing herself"? Is it "getting her ideas out there"?

Or is it something else?

I'm going to do a little self-examination on this subject, which I think is pretty critical in this era of the web, Amazon, print-on-demand, and instant and easy self-publishing, these days when literally a million new books (700,000 self-published, 300,000 traditionally published) appear each year. How do we—you and I—navigate those waters, not just financially or professionally but psychologically, emotionally, spiritually?

2
BEING IGNORED

If you're a working writer struggling to get published (or published again) or wrestling with the utility or non-utility of self-publishing, you may log on to my blog, www.stevenpressfield.com, and think, *Oh, Pressfield's got it made; he's had real-world success; he's a brand.*

Trust me. It ain't necessarily so.

I don't expect to be reviewed by *The New York Times*. Ever. The last time was 1998 for *Gates of Fire*. *The War of Art* was never reviewed. *The Lion's Gate* never. My other seven novels never.

My most recent novel, *The Knowledge*, was reviewed nowhere by no one.

If I want to retain my sanity, I have to banish that way of thinking from my psyche. I cannot permit my professional or artistic self-conception to be dependent on external validation, at least not of the mainstream recognition variety.

It's never gonna happen.

I'm never going to get it.

If you're not reviewed by *The New York Times* (or seen on *Oprah*), your book will have tough, tough sledding to gain awareness in the marketplace. No book I publish under Black Irish is going to achieve wide awareness. BI's reach is too tiny. Our penetration of the marketplace is too miniscule. And even being published by one of the Big Five, as *The Lion's Gate* was by Penguin in 2014, is only marginally more effective.

There are maybe a hundred writers of fiction whose new books will be reviewed with any broad reach in the mainstream press. Jonathan Franzen, Stephen King, J.K. Rowling, etc. I'm not on that list. My stuff will never receive that kind of attention.

Does that bother me? I'd be a liar if I said I didn't want to be recognized or at least have my existence and my work acknowledged.

But reality is reality. As Garth on Wayne's World once said of his own butt, "Accept it before it destroys you."

It's curiously empowering to grasp this and to accept it.

It's truth.

It's reality.

It forces you to ask, *Why am I writing?*

What is important to me?

What am I in this for?

Here is novelist Neal Stephenson from his short essay, "Why I Am a Bad Correspondent":

Another factor in this choice [to focus entirely on writing to the exclusion of other "opportunities" and distractions] is that writing fiction every day seems to be an essential component in my sustaining good mental health. If I get blocked from writing fiction, I rapidly become depressed, and extremely unpleasant to be around. As long as I keep writing it, though, I am fit to be around other people. So all of the incentives point in the direction of devoting all available hours to fiction writing.

I asked hypothetically in chapter 1: What if a writer worked her entire life, produced a worthy and original body of work, yet had never been published by a mainstream press and had never achieved conventional recognition? Would her literary efforts have been in vain? Would she be considered a "failure"?

Part of my own answer arises from Neal Stephenson's observation above.

I wrote for twenty-eight years before I got a novel published. I can't tell you how many times friends, family members, lovers, and spouses implored me for my own sake to wake up and face reality.

I couldn't.

Because my reality was not *The New York Times* or the bestseller list or even simply getting an agent and having a meeting with somebody. My reality was, *If I stop writing I will have to kill myself.*

I'm compelled.

I have no choice.

I don't know why I was born like this. I don't know what it means. I can't tell you if it's crazy or deluded or even evil.

I have to keep trying.

That pile of unpublished manuscripts in my closet may seem to you (and to me too) to be a monument to folly and self-delusion. But I'm gonna keep adding to it, whether HarperCollins gives a shit, or *The New Yorker*, or even my cat who's perched beside me right now on my desktop.

I am a writer.

I was born to do this.

I have no choice.

3
WHAT WORKS AND WHAT DOESN'T

I wrote in the preceding chapter that I would have to kill myself if I couldn't write. That wasn't hyperbole.

Here, in no particular order, are the activities and aspirations that don't work for me (and I've tried them all extensively, as I imagine you may have too if you're reading this book).

Money doesn't work.

Success.

Family life, domestic bliss, service to country, dedication to a cause, however selfless or noble.

None of these works for me.

Identity association of all kinds (religious, political, cultural, national) is meaningless to me. Sex provides no lasting relief. Nor do the ready forms of self-administered distraction—drugs and alcohol, travel, life on the web.

Fashion and style don't work, though I agree they're pretty cool. Reading used to help and still does on occasion. Art indeed, but only up to a point.

It doesn't work for me to teach or to labor selflessly for others. I can't be a farmer or drive a truck. I've tried. My friend Jeff jokingly claims that his goal is world domination. That wouldn't work for me either.

I can't find peace of mind as a warrior or an athlete or by leading an organization. Fame means nothing. Attention and praise are nice but hollow. "Winning Wimbledon," as Chris Evert once said, "lasts about an hour."

Meditation and spiritual practice, however much I admire the path and those who follow it, don't work for me.

The only thing that allows me to sit quietly in the evening is the completion of a worthy day's work. What work? The labor of entering my imagination and trying to come back out with something that is worthy both of my own time and effort and of the time and effort of my brothers and sisters to read it or watch it or listen to it.

That's my drug. That's what keeps me sane.

I'm not saying this way of life is wholesome or balanced. It's not. It's certainly not "normal." By no means would I recommend it as a course to emulate.

Nor did I choose this path for myself, either consciously or deliberately. I came to it at the end of a long dark tunnel and then only as the last recourse, the thing I'd been avoiding all my life.

When I see people, friends even, destroy their lives with pills or booze or domestic violence or any of the thousand ways a person can face-plant himself or herself into nonexistence, I feel nothing but compassion. I understand how hard the road is, and how lightless. I'm a whisker away from hitting that ditch myself.

The Muse saved me. I offer thanks to the goddess every day for beating the hell out of me until I finally heeded and took up her cause.

No one will ever say it better than Henry Miller did in *Tropic of Capricorn:*

> I reached out for something to attach myself to—and I found nothing. But in reaching out, in the effort to grasp, to attach myself, left high and dry as I was, I nevertheless found something I had not looked for—*myself.* I found that what I had desired all my life was not to live—if what others are doing is called living—but to express myself. I realized that I had never had the least interest in living, but only in this which I am doing now, something which is parallel to life, of it at the same time, and beyond it. What is true interests me scarcely at all, nor even what is real; only that interests me which I imagine to be, that which I had stifled every day in order to live.

4
WRITING "AS IF"

The hippie version of behavioral therapy (I remember it well) was Acting "As If."

Are you scared? Are you anxious? Act *as if* you're not.

Shawn has a principle for Black Irish Books: publish as if. In other words, bring out a book/promote it etc. *as if* we were Knopf, as if we were Random House.

What about writing as if?

Remember, the title of this little book is *Why Write?* It's my own admittedly personal, idiosyncratic, possibly demented view of why I do what I do.

I definitely write as if.

I write as if I'm being published by Knopf/Harper-Collins, Penguin Random House/Simon & Schuster/Hachette/Little, Brown.

I write as if my stuff is gonna be reviewed by *The New York Times*, *The New Yorker*, *The Times* of London.

I write as if the Nobel Prize committee will check every comma.

I write as if Steven Spielberg will be personally eye-balling an advance reading copy.

I write as if people will be reading my work five hundred years from now (assuming of course that planet Earth is still inhabited by humans).

More important than all of the above, I write as if the Muse herself will be going over my stuff. I don't want her saying, "*This* is what I gave you?"

When I was writing *Gates of Fire*, the criterion I applied was, "If the actual three hundred Spartans were reading this on the far shore of the river Styx, would they say, 'Yeah, you got it reasonably right?'"

But let's take this line of action to a deeper level.

You and I as writers must write as if we were highly paid, even though we may not be.

We must write as if we were top-shelf literary professionals, even though we may not (yet) be.

We must write as if we were being held to the highest standards of truth, of vision, of scale, of imagination, even though we may not be.

We must write as if our works mattered, even though they may not.

As if they will make a difference, even though they may not.

As if our lives and our sanity depended on it. Because, believe me, they do.

To say that we write (or live) "as if" is another way of saying we have turned pro.

We are operating as professionals.

We are in this for keeps.

We are in it for the long haul.

We are committed.

We are warriors.

We are for real.

Behold, I send you forth as sheep in the midst of wolves; be ye therefore wise as serpents, and harmless as doves ... ye shall be brought before governors and kings for my sake ... but when they deliver you up, take no thought how or what ye shall speak; for it shall be given you in that same hour what ye shall speak.

There is great wisdom in acting as if and writing as if.

Is life without meaning? Are you and I adrift on a speck of dust hurtling in the dark through a pointless cosmos?

Maybe.

But we can't act that way.

We must act as if there were meaning, as if our lives and actions did have significance, as if love is real and death is an illusion, as if the future will be better than the past, whatever that means.

One of Seth Godin's great contributions is the idea of "picking yourself." Don't sit on a stool like Lana Turner at Schwab's Drugstore in Hollywood, waiting to be discovered by some movie mogul and made into the next big star.

Pick yourself.

Act as if you were a pro, a homerun hitter, the real thing.

There's additional magic to the practice of acting as if and writing as if. In some crazy way, acting and writing as if makes our beliefs about ourselves come true.

What we had only projected inevitably takes on its own reality.

"You're an actress," Art Carney says to Lily Tomlin at a scary moment in Robert Benton's great private eye flick *The Late Show*. "Act brave."

5
THE MUSE AND ME

We were talking in chapter 3 about "what works and what doesn't," i.e., what activities produce (for me) peace of mind at the end of the day. I listed a number that didn't work—money, attention, family life, etc.

Let's talk today about what does work.

If you asked me at this time of my life to define my identity—after cycling through many, many over the years—I would say I am a servant of the Muse.

That's what I do.

That's how I live my life.

Consider, for perspective, this incomplete and possibly out-of-order selection from our newest Nobel laureate.

Bob Dylan
The Freewheelin' Bob Dylan
The Times They Are a-Changin'
Highway 61 Revisited
Blonde on Blonde
Bringing It All Back Home
Blood on the Tracks
Desire
John Wesley Harding
Street-Legal

Nashville Skyline
Slow Train Coming
Hard Rain
Time Out of Mind
Tempest
Shadows in the Night

See the Muse in there? Mr. D might not agree with the terminology I'm employing, but he is definitely *serving something*, isn't he? Something is leading him and he is following it.

That's exactly what I do.

An idea seizes me. *Gates of Fire. Bagger Vance. The Lion's Gate.* Where is this idea coming from? The unconscious? The soul? The Jungian "Self"?

My answer: the Muse.

I experience this apparition-of-the-idea as *an assignment.* I'm being tasked by the Muse with a mission.

> You are to travel by sea to Antioch. There you
> will meet a tall man with one eye who will hand
> you a talisman ....

My instinctive reaction, always, is to reject the idea. "It's too hard. Nobody's gonna be interested in it. I'm not the right person, etc."

This of course is Resistance.

In Hero's Journey terms, it's "Refusal of the Call."

In a few days (or weeks or months) I recognize this.

I accept my task.

I accede to my mission.

This is how I live my life. From project to project, year by year. As the Plains Indians followed the herds of buffalo and the seasonal grass, I follow the Muse.

Wherever she tells me to go, I go.

Whatever she asks me to do, I do.

I fear the Muse. She has slapped me around a few times over the years. I've been scared straight.

She has also cared for me. She has never failed me, never been untrue to me, never led me in any direction except that which was best for me on the deepest possible level.

She has taken me to places I would never have gone without her. She has shown me parts of the world, and parts of myself, that I would never have seen, had she not led me there.

But let's take this notion a little deeper.

What I'm really saying is that I believe life exists on at least two levels. The lower level is the material plane. That's where you and I live. The higher level is the home of the soul, the *neshama*, the Muse.

The higher level is a lot smarter than the lower level.

The higher level understands life in a far, far deeper way.

It understands who we are.

It understands why we are here.

It understands the past and the future and our roles within both.

My job, as I understand it, is to make myself open to this higher level.

My job is to keep myself alert and receptive.

My job is to be ready, in the fullest professional sense, when the alarm bell goes off and I have to slide down the pole and jump into the fire engine.

Again, I didn't choose this way of living.

I didn't seek it out.

I didn't even know it existed.

I tried everything else and nothing else succeeded. This was the only thing I've found that works for me.

In other words, I don't do what I do for money. I don't do it for ego or attention or because I think it's cool. I don't do it because I have a message to deliver or because I want to influence my brothers and sisters in any way (other than to let them know, from my point of view anyway, that they are not alone in their struggle).

When I say I'm a servant of the Muse, I mean that literally.

The goddess has saved my life and given it meaning or, perhaps more accurately, she has allowed me to participate in the meaning she already embodies, whether I understand it or not.

Everything I do in my life is a form of getting ready for the next assignment.

6
THE INNER JOURNEY

I wouldn't blame anyone who read the preceding chapter and thought, "Man, that's a bit airy-fairy, ain't it?"

Lemme answer by getting even more airy-fairy.

Consider this artist's body of work:

Goodbye, Columbus
Letting Go
Portnoy's Complaint
The Great American Novel
My Life as a Man
The Professor of Desire
The Ghost Writer
Zuckerman Unbound
The Anatomy Lesson
The Counterlife
Sabbath's Theater
American Pastoral
I Married a Communist
The Human Stain
The Dying Animal
The Plot Against America

Clearly there's a theme here, isn't there. Clearly Philip Roth is dealing with a specific, discrete issue. He's examining this theme from every angle, playing games with it, turning it inside-out and upside-down.

How about this artist?

Greetings from Asbury Park, N.J.
The Wild, the Innocent & the E Street Shuffle
Born to Run
Darkness on the Edge of Town
The River
Nebraska
Born in the U.S.A.
Tunnel of Love
Human Touch
Lucky Town
The Ghost of Tom Joad
Working on a Dream
Wrecking Ball
High Hopes
Springsteen on Broadway

The Muse's fingerprints, to me, are all over both these bodies of work.

Let's ask why.

What's her purpose? Why is she doing this? We can agree, can't we, that the world is a better place because Philip Roth wrote the books he wrote and Bruce Springsteen recorded the songs he recorded?

So something positive is going on.

Why did *American Pastoral* come after *Zuckerman Unbound*? Why did *Born in the U.S.A.* follow *Darkness on the Edge of Town* and *The River*?

The artists are evolving, aren't they?

Why didn't Philip Roth write *Beloved* or *The Color Purple*? Why didn't the Boss record *Blood on the Tracks*?

Each of these souls, if you ask me, is on a journey. Just like I am and just like you are. If we're artists, the works we produce are the material articulations of that journey.

The journey itself is interior.

The journey takes place within the soul.

The Muse gives us works to bring into being in the same way and for the same purpose that the unconscious sends us dreams.

Each work is a message in a bottle from the higher level—our soul, our Self, our being-in-potential—to our stumbling, struggling incarnations here on the material plane.

Can we say that Philip Roth and Bruce Springsteen as artists have led fulfilled lives? Maybe we can't bet the ranch on it, but it sure looks like they've done pretty well.

For sure we have to give it to them that they've followed their stars. They've been true over long careers to their most profound internal callings.

In other words, if you ask me, the Muse is not just giving us as artists the works we produce.

She's guiding our souls' journeys.

She's our mentor and our navigator.

Have we entered this life as the most recent in an extended succession of incarnations?

Will we re-appear at some later time in another life?

Will the theme of our current and prior lives carry over?

Will Philip Roth and Bruce Springsteen, in some transfigured forms, continue to "work on" the issues that have possessed each of them in this lifetime?

[I told ya this chapter was gonna get even more airy-fairy.]

7
GET IN THE CAB

One of my favorite passages from books about the artist's life is this one from Twyla Tharp's *The Creative Habit*:

> I begin each day of my life with a ritual: I wake up at 5:30 a.m., put on my workout clothes, my leg warmers, my sweatshirts, and my hat. I walk outside my Manhattan home, hail a taxi, and tell the driver to take me to the Pumping Iron gym at 91st Street and First Avenue, where I work out for two hours. The ritual is not the stretching and weight training I put my body through each morning at the gym; the ritual is the cab. The moment I tell the driver where to go I have completed the ritual.

There is great wisdom to Ms. Tharp's ritual/habit. The key phrase is " ... the ritual is not the gym ... the ritual is the cab."

In other words, it's the practice, not the product.

What counts is not "Did I come up with a great dance breakthrough today?" What counts is "Did I do my practice today?"

What does it mean to "have a practice"?

We think of that phrase usually in terms of yoga, say, or the martial arts or other spiritual pursuits.

"I have a yoga practice."

"I have a meditation practice."

Twyla Tharp has a dance practice.

Or more accurately, she has an artistic practice.

A creativity practice.

You and I have a writing practice.

As I turns out, I start my day exactly like Twyla Tharp. Except I live in Los Angeles, so I don't hail a cab or an Uber to go to the gym. I drive. But, like Ms. Tharp, my practice starts the instant I roll out of bed.

I am getting ready for the Muse.

My goal for that day—and every day—is not to kick ass at the keyboard or solve Narrative Problem #27 or lick Act Two.

My goal is to do my practice.

A practice is life-long.

A practice is not about "results." It's about the doing.

Starting the day (for me) at the gym is about seeking the proper mindset.

I'm rehearsing.

I'm rehearsing being focused.

I'm rehearsing the confrontation with Resistance.

I'm rehearsing humility.

I'm rehearsing aggressiveness.

Like Twyla Tharp, I'm practicing for the studio.

The finish, it turns out, is as important as the start.

When Ms. Tharp catches a cab home from her dance studio, I know a part of her mind is getting ready for tomorrow. She's rehearsing pulling on her sweats, riding the elevator downstairs, stepping into the street and raising her right hand.

A practice is life-long.

The point is to do it today and do it tomorrow and do it the next day.

The Muse is watching Ms. Tharp, just like she's watching you and she's watching me. Call it the unconscious if you like. The Self. The soul.

That part of us that knows us better than we know ourselves.

That part that understands our calling.

That part that holds the works-in-potential that we will transform into works-in-reality.

The Muse likes to see Twyla hailing that cab.

On Ms. Tharp's Manhattan block there may be a hundred, five hundred other aspiring artists, dancers, writers, filmmakers, entrepreneurs.

Which one do you think the Muse favors at 5:30 in the morning?

A final sidebar: I used to drive a cab in New York City. Had I known of Twyla Tharp's pre-dawn ritual, I would've found out where she lived and parked my taxi outside her building every morning. I would've made sure that I was the dude who took her to the gym.

I have a feeling she's a big tipper.

8
SIX YEARS IN THE LIFE

I was thinking about Marco Rubio.

I'm writing this a few days before the 2016 election, so I don't know if he won his Senate race or not, but let's assume for the sake of argument that he did.

I'll bet Marco and his family are breathing a major sigh of relief. A Senate term runs six years. The Rubios are now set up till 2022.

No worries about fading from the public scene. No shilling for work in the private sector. Marco now, and for the next six years, possesses a position of high status and influence, a guaranteed income, an externally imposed structure of order and significance. He's got a place to go to every morning. The position even comes with a hopeful future. It confers a six-year tenure for its holder to work toward his next incarnation—another presidential run, whatever.

Marco Rubio is locked in, safe and solid, for the next six years.

What about you and me?

What about us as artists and entrepreneurs?

What do our next six years look like, lacking any and all of the perks and advantages that Marco's got?

You and I possess no guaranteed income. We own no position of power and influence, no staff, no office, no free government car or expense account. We have no workplace to go to in the morning, no schedule of meetings and hearings and fact-finding excursions, no built-in structure to shape our days.

We're on our own. We can drop dead in the middle of Main Street and passersby will be stepping over our corpses.

Whatever meaning and significance our lives may bring forth, we have to create it all by ourselves.

On the other hand, consider these six years:

Clouds
Ladies of the Canyon
Blue
For the Roses
Court and Spark
The Hissing of Summer Lawns

(Specifically: "Chelsea Morning", "Both Sides Now", "Big Yellow Taxi", "Woodstock", "The Circle Game", "My Old Man", "Blue", "A Case of You", "Barangrill", "You Turn Me On I'm a Radio", "Blonde in the Bleachers", "Help Me", "Free Man in Paris", "People's Parties", "Car on a Hill", "Down to You", "Just Like This Train", "Trouble Child", "Twisted", "Sweet Bird", "Shadows and Light".)

Or how about this artist/entrepreneur:

Yoyodyne
Permission marketing
eMarketing
Purple Cow
All Marketers Are Liars
The Dip
Tribes
Squidoo

I'm fudging a little on dates here, but you get the idea. Seth Godin had a pretty decent Senate term, didn't he?

Or how about this dude, in just *one* year?

Photovoltaic Effect
Brownian Motion
Theory of Special Relativity
$E=mc^2$
Mass-energy Equivalence

The Muse is an amazing gal, isn't she? She can reach down to you and me (or reach *up*, if you'd prefer to think of it that way, from our unconscious, our self, our neshama) and supply all the structure, power, creativity, significance, meaning, and fun that any of our fellows might get from a job, a posting, an externally imposed order of daily life.

Can anybody look at the bodies of work of [fill in the blank: any artist, entrepreneur, writer, filmmaker, photographer, software designer, you name it] and say there is no meaning in the universe, no order, no evolution, no progress?

Our job, yours and mine, is 1) to make ourselves open to whatever portion of that invisible force has been set aside for us alone (and believe me, that portion is there, with our names on it) and 2) to make ourselves ready in terms of skills, knowledge of craft, professionalism, and capacity to manage our internal impulses—positive as well as negative—so that we can convert the Muse's gifts into works that are accessible to our brothers and sisters.

We asked at the start of this little book, "What if an artist produced over her lifetime an original and authentic body of work, but that production had never been recognized widely among her contemporaries? Would we say that her work had been in vain?"

Again I say no.

That body of work has been her artist's journey, her destiny as a soul. The realization of that inspiration of the Muse (in other words, its transformation from the invisible state of pure potential to its realized state as material works of art) is as valid a life's work as raising a family, selflessly serving one's people or nation or planet, or achieving any kind of conventional recognition or fame.

By producing that work, by following her star, our hypothetical artist has lived as realized a life as an oak that has grown to its full height and breadth, a sperm whale that has circled the globe as a matriarch of her ocean-depths clan, or a comet that has lapped the solar system and is banking around to do it again.

And she knows it, our artist.

She may not have had a Capitol Hill office to go to every morning, or been greeted as "Madame Senator" as she went about her day. But she has been as true to her deepest internal calling as Joni Mitchell and Seth Godin and Albert Einstein.

And I'll tell you something else. Someday, and maybe much sooner than she or we imagine, that body of work *will be* recognized beyond her small inner circle.

Soul has power.

Its light cannot remain unseen forever.

9
WHAT KIND OF WRITER ARE YOU?

I had been working in Hollywood for five or six years and had a semi-respectable B-level screenwriting career going, when I got a new agent. My new agent was a go-getter. He decided to mount a campaign where he would "re-introduce me to the town."

That sounded good to me.

My new agent started setting me up with meetings. The campaign would last six weeks, he said. He would send me out to two or three places a week—studios, production companies, the individual development entities of actors, directors, etc.

The meetings would usually last between half an hour and an hour. They were meet-and-greets, friendly, informal. It would be me and two or three development execs.

The company people would tell me what they were looking for and I would tell them what I was working on. For example, if it was the production company of an actor, the execs might say, "Jim's looking for something darker than his usual stuff, something David Fincher-esque, with a real edge to it." Or I might say, "I just finished a spec Western" or pitch them a supernatural thriller I had percolating inside me. The hope was that

31

the twain would meet and a gig would come out of it, or maybe I would sell one of my specs.

And for the first couple of weeks, everything was going great. The meetings had energy; plans were made; I was doing callbacks and follow-ups.

The only problem was I getting depressed.

I mean down.

Clinically down.

Three weeks became four. My tally was up around ten, twelve meetings.

I was getting seriously bummed and I couldn't figure out why.

I got to dreading these meetings.

What was wrong with me?

Why was this experience such a bringdown?

My bummed state seemed to make no sense. The people I was meeting with were universally smart, dedicated, enthusiastic. They knew movies. They liked me. I liked them.

What was my problem?

Slowly the answer began to dawn on me.

Floating in the air in each meeting was an unspoken assumption. Everybody in the room believed this assumption. This assumption was the foundation of everything that the studio and development people said and did.

It was assumed as well that I, by virtue of being in these meetings of my own free will, accepted this assumption too.

The assumption was this:

We will do anything for a hit.

The goal was box office. A winner at any cost. Short of producing a snuff flick, the name of the game was commercial success.

Who could argue with that, right?

Hollywood is a business. That's why they call it "the industry."

The problem was I didn't accept that assumption.

It wasn't my assumption.

I didn't buy into it at all.

I wanted to write what I wanted to write. What I cared about was whatever idea seized my imagination. I wanted to have a hit, sure, but out of a hundred potential writing ideas, there were at least eighty I wouldn't touch, no matter how much you paid me or how sure-fire they were at producing a hit.

They just weren't interesting to me.

It struck me that I might be in career trouble.

I was actually getting scared.

I realized that I wasn't in the same business as the executives I was meeting with.

They were looking for one thing and I was looking for another.

In other words, for the first time in my twenty-plus year writing life, I found myself confronting the questions, "What kind of writer am I? Why am I doing this?

How do I define success as a writer?"

Am I a writer for hire?

Am I a genre writer?

What kind of writer am I?

And more important: Am I in the right business? Is there a future for me here?

OMG, at forty-three years old am I gonna have to re-invent myself yet again? As what?

Here was the conceptual breakthrough that solved the problem (at least for the moment):

I visualized two circles.

One circle was "Movie ideas the industry wants to make."

The other was "Movie ideas I want to write."

The two circles might not coincide, one on top of the other. They might in fact barely overlap at all. But there was *some* overlap, however small.

I told myself, "I will make my living in that overlap."

And it worked.

For another five or six years, for six or seven screen-plays (most unproduced but all written to a paycheck), this new theory worked fine.

The problem was I had opened a kind of Pandora's box by asking those questions, "What kind of writer am I? What is my objective? How do I define writerly success for myself?"

The answers eventually took me out of the movie biz.

What kind of writer are you?

Why are you pursuing a literary vocation?

How would you define success for yourself?

Are you in the writing biz for money? Fame? Recognition?

Are you trying to prove to your father/mother/ex-spouse that you're not a bum and a loser?

Do you have a message to deliver?

A plan for world domination?

Are you writing because it beats working in a coal mine?

If your fondest hopes for your writing career were realized, what would those results look like?

Who would you be?

Where would you be?

What would you be?

What works would you have produced?

What reception—commercially, artistically, politically—would these works have generated?

If you knew, right now, that this happy ending would never be realized, would you still keep writing?

How compelled are you to pursue this vocation?

Is it a livelihood? A craft? A passion? An obsession?

These are questions that you and I have to ask and answer, no matter how uncomfortable they make us feel or how much we'd prefer to avoid them entirely. For me, the process was life-altering and life-enhancing. These questions and the answers they elicited helped me not only to advance along the path I had embarked on years earlier, blindly and impulsively, but also to see that path clearly and to understand it (or begin to understand it) truly for the first time.

What kind of writer are you?

ABOUT THE AUTHOR

STEVEN PRESSFIELD is the bestselling author of *The Legend of Bagger Vance, Gates of Fire, The Afghan Campaign,* and *The Lion's Gate,* as well as the cult classics on creativity, *The War of Art, Turning Pro, Do the Work,* and *Nobody Wants to Read Your Sh*t.*

His Wednesday column on www.StevenPressfield.com is among the most popular writing blogs on the web.

facebook.com/StevePressfield

twitter.com/spressfield